LeSean McCoy

By Jon M. Fishman

AMAZING ATHLETES

Lerner Publications ◆ Minneapolis

Lerner Publications Company
A division of Lerner Publishing Group, Inc.
241 First Avenue North
Minneapolis, MN 55401 USA

For reading levels and more information, look up this title at www.lernerbooks.com.

Library of Congress Cataloging-in-Publication Data

Fishman, Jon M.
    LeSean McCoy / by Jon M. Fishman.
      pages cm. — (Amazing athletes)
    Includes index.
    ISBN 978-1-4677-7920-3 (lb : alk. paper) — ISBN 978-1-4677-8111-4 (pb : alk. paper) —
ISBN 978-1-4677-8544-0 (eb pdf)
    1. McCoy, LeSean—Juvenile literature 2. Football players—United States—Biography—Juvenile
literature. I. Title.
GV939.A54F57 2015
796.33092—dc23 [B]   2015012384

Manufactured in the United States of America
1 – BP – 7/15/15

TABLE OF CONTENTS

LeSean McCoy runs down the field gaining yardage against the Dallas Cowboys.

BEING HIMSELF

Philadelphia Eagles **running back** LeSean McCoy took the ball and hopped to his left. Then he cut right as a **linebacker** sailed by. LeSean leaned forward to gain an extra yard as he crashed to the ground in a heap of players.

LeSean and the Eagles were playing against the Dallas Cowboys on November 27, 2014. The fans at the stadium near Dallas were fired up. With only five games left to play in the season, the Eagles claimed first place in their **division**. But the Cowboys trailed the Eagles by just one game.

The Philadelphia Eagles played against the Dallas Cowboys at AT&T Stadium in Arlington, Texas.

The Eagles led the Cowboys in the third quarter, 23–10. Philadelphia **quarterback** Mark Sanchez handed the ball to LeSean. The running back stormed to his left for seven yards. Two plays later, Sanchez gave the ball to LeSean again. This time, the hard-to-catch runner headed up the middle of the field. He pushed a defender away with his left arm.

LeSean fights through a tackle.

Then he ran past another Cowboys player who tried to tackle him. LeSean was in the clear! He kept running and raised his arms as he crossed the **goal line**. It was a 38-yard touchdown!

The Eagles and Cowboys have played against each other 112 times. The Cowboys have won 63 of those games, while the Eagles have won just 49.

LeSean scores a touchdown.

Philadelphia kicked a **field goal** in the fourth quarter and won the game, 33–10. LeSean had run for 159 yards. The win was a huge step on the road to the **playoffs** for the Eagles.

The year before, LeSean had run for the most

Eagles fans cheer for LeSean and his teammates.

LeSean celebrates with teammates after the game.

rushing yards in the NFL. In 2014, he was near the top of the list again. But LeSean doesn't focus on winning awards or proving he's the best. "I just try to be me," he said after the game.

LeSean was raised in Harrisburg, Pennsylvania.

WONDER KID

On July 12, 1988, LeSean Kamel McCoy was born in Harrisburg, Pennsylvania. He lived with his father, Ron, and his mother, Daphne. LeSean has a brother named LeRon.

LeSean is five years younger than LeRon. The younger boy looked up to his big brother.

LeSean wanted to do whatever LeRon was doing. LeRon often played football with his friends. "We all played tackle [football]," LeRon said. "And even though [LeSean] was five years younger, he had to play [tackle] too."

Playing with the older boys made LeSean tough. And he was full of energy. Ron and Daphne signed him up for a youth football league. "We wanted to get all that energy out," Ron said.

Like these boys, LeSean started playing football at a young age.

By the time LeSean was 11 years old, he was well known in Harrisburg as a good football player. Coaches from two local high schools began asking LeRon about his younger brother. One of these schools, Bishop McDevitt High School, is a private school. The other, Harrisburg High School (HHS), is a public school. They are fierce **rivals** on the football field. Both schools wanted LeSean on their team.

Daphne gave LeSean the nickname Shady to describe his personality. She said her son can be moody at times.

The McCoys decided to send their boys to McDevitt. To pay for the school, both parents held jobs. With only one car in the family, Daphne and Ron drove each other to and from work each day. They taught LeSean and LeRon to work hard and to save their money.

LeSean made an instant impact on the McDevitt football team. He darted around the field with the ball. He made smart decisions about where to run. LeSean had all the moves. He cut to his left and to his right. He spun and ducked and shoved to avoid tacklers.

As a junior in 2004, LeSean put together one of the greatest seasons in Pennsylvania high school football history. In 13 games, he scored 31 touchdowns. He averaged more than 217 rushing yards per game. That season made college **scouts** around the country take notice.

The Arizona Cardinals play at University of Phoenix Stadium.

HIGHS AND LOWS

After high school, LeSean's older brother, LeRon, had gone on to play **wide receiver** at Indiana University of Pennsylvania. In 2005, he entered the NFL **draft**. He was chosen by the Arizona Cardinals. LeSean visited his brother in Arizona and liked what he saw. The younger player was impressed with LeRon's house and the NFL lifestyle. "All of this is what I want," LeSean told his mother. "I'm going to get it."

LeSean was well on his way to playing in the NFL. In 2005, he was one of the top-ranked high school players in the United States. The senior received dozens of college **scholarship** offers. College is an important step for athletes who want to play in the NFL. But before LeSean could choose a college, he had to play his senior season of high school football.

LeSean's brother, LeRon (right), played for the Arizona Cardinals.

LeRon didn't play in the NFL for long. He played just 10 games for the Cardinals and scored one touchdown.

McDevitt's fourth game of the year was against rival HHS. Late in the game, LeSean took the ball up the middle of the field. He was tackled and didn't get up.

LeSean's ankle was broken. It was a severe injury called a **compound fracture**.

Before the injury, LeSean had been on pace for an incredible season. In just four games, he had rushed for 889 yards and 10 touchdowns. But now that LeSean had a broken ankle, his season was over. It was possible he would never play football again.

Compound fractures are serious injuries.

LeSean was upset. "I didn't want to go to school," he said. "I felt like my identity was gone." The injury caused most colleges to withdraw their scholarship offers to LeSean. He graduated from McDevitt in 2006 with an uncertain football future.

LeSean's ankle healed and grew strong. To help rebuild his value as a football player, he decided to spend a year at Milford Academy in New Berlin, New York. Milford is a school that prepares students for college. In 10 games with the Milford football team, LeSean rushed for only 547 yards and scored four touchdowns. He didn't run with the same confidence that he had before the injury.

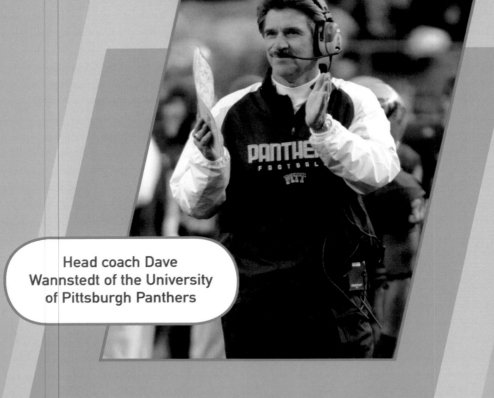

Head coach Dave Wannstedt of the University of Pittsburgh Panthers

COMEBACK

A few people believed that LeSean could still be a good college running back. One of those people was Dave Wannstedt of the University of Pittsburgh. The head coach of the Pitt Panthers football team had followed LeSean's **career** for years. He decided to offer LeSean a place on his team. "I'll give you a chance to get your name back," Wannstedt said. LeSean cried with happiness.

In 2007, LeSean proved that his ankle injury was completely behind him. He played in 12 games with the Panthers. He racked up 1,328 rushing yards and ran for 14 touchdowns. Those were the third-best totals for any rusher in the Big East **Conference** that season.

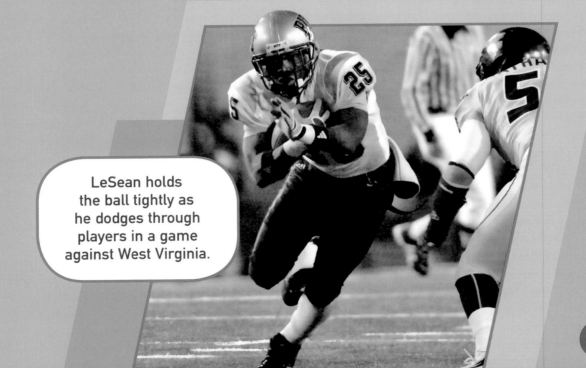

LeSean holds the ball tightly as he dodges through players in a game against West Virginia.

He also caught a touchdown pass. In 2008, LeSean was even better. In 13 games, he totaled 1,488 rushing yards, the second-best in the Big East that year. He also scored 21

LeSean scores a touchdown during a game against the Bowling Green Falcons in 2008.

rushing touchdowns. That was more than any other runner in the conference.

After the 2008 season, many scouts believed LeSean was ready for the next level of football. He thought about leaving Pitt for the NFL. It was a chance to reach the goal he had dreamed about since visiting LeRon in Arizona years ago.

LeSean also thought about his high school ankle injury. He knew he might not always be healthy enough to play football. "Nothing is promised to us and it can all be taken away in a moment," he said. LeSean decided to enter the 2009 NFL draft. The Eagles chose him in the second round.

Before games, LeSean likes to listen to hip-hop artists such as 50 Cent and Jay Z.

Many NFL teams are cautious with their **rookies** and don't allow them to play much. Teams want to give new players time to adjust to football's highest level. But the Eagles didn't hold LeSean back. In 2009, he carried the ball 155 times. That was twice as many carries as the next running back on the team. He gained 637 yards and punched in four touchdowns. It was the start of something big for LeSean and Philadelphia.

LeSean warms up before a game against the Miami Dolphins.

SHADY IN THE SPOTLIGHT

In 2010, LeSean led the Eagles in carries again. This time, he collected 1,080 yards and nine touchdowns. He wowed fans with his quick cuts and incredible ability to avoid being tackled.

Both fans and fellow players saw that

LeSean had the talent to become one of the best running backs in the NFL. In 2011, that's just what he did. He racked up yards and touchdowns all season. In the third quarter of a game against the New York Jets, LeSean took the handoff. He skipped to his right and danced into the **end zone**. It was the 19th touchdown of the year for LeSean, the most in Eagles history.

LeSean snatches the ball during a game against the New York Jets.

He scored his 20th touchdown later in the game. LeSean finished the season with 1,309 rushing yards. That was the fourth-best mark in the NFL in 2011.

LeSean celebrates after a touchdown in 2011.

The next season, LeSean missed four games with injuries. He still managed to gain 840 rushing yards for the year. Then, in 2013, LeSean racked up 1,607 rushing yards. It was the best total in the NFL. That made LeSean the first Philadelphia player to lead the NFL in rushing yards since 1949.

LeSean runs through a tackle.

In 2014, LeSean continued to break records. In a December game against the Seattle Seahawks, he gained his 6,539th career NFL rushing yard. This total made him the Eagles all-time leading rusher. After just six seasons with the team, setting this record was a

Wilbert Montgomery *(left)* held the Eagles touchdown record in 1979 before LeSean broke it.

startling feat. Unfortunately, Philadelphia lost three of their final four games in 2014 and didn't make the playoffs.

Since breaking his ankle in high school, LeSean has savored every success on the football field. After all,

LeSean and his son, LeSean McCoy Jr., pose with his jersey in 2015.

his career almost ended just as it was starting. After the 2014 season, LeSean was surprised when the Eagles traded him to the Buffalo Bills.

LeSean signs autographs for fans after a game.

He had never played for a professional football team based outside of Pennsylvania before. But it didn't take long for him to settle in with the Bills. "I can't wait to get to work," LeSean said.

Selected Career Highlights

2014 Ran for 1,319 yards and scored five touchdowns with the Eagles
Set the Eagles all-time record for rushing yards in a career
Voted to the NFL Pro Bowl for the third time

2013 Ran for 1,607 yards and scored 11 touchdowns with the Eagles
Claimed the NFL rushing yards title
Voted to the NFL Pro Bowl for the second time

2012 Ran for 840 yards and scored five touchdowns with the Eagles

2011 Ran for 1,309 yards and scored 20 touchdowns with the Eagles
Set the Eagles all-time record for touchdowns in a season
Voted to the NFL Pro Bowl for the first time

2010 Ran for 1,080 yards and scored nine touchdowns with the Eagles

2009 Chosen by the Eagles with the 53rd overall pick in the NFL draft
Ran for 637 yards and scored four touchdowns in the first season with the Eagles

2008 Ran for 1,488 yards and scored 21 touchdowns with the University of Pittsburgh

2007 Ran for 1,328 yards and scored 15 touchdowns with the University of Pittsburgh

2006 Graduated from Bishop McDevitt High School
Ran for 547 yards and scored four touchdowns with Milford Academy

2005 Ran for 889 yards and scored 10 touchdowns with Bishop McDevitt High School
Broke his ankle during the fourth game of the season with Bishop McDevitt High School

2004 Ran for 2,828 yards and scored 31 touchdowns with Bishop McDevitt High School

Glossary

career: a job that someone does for a long time

compound fracture: a broken bone that sticks out through the skin

conference: a group of divisions of sports teams that play against one another

division: a group of teams that play against one another. Division winners move on to the playoffs.

draft: a yearly event in which teams take turns choosing new players from a group

end zone: the area beyond the goal line at each end of a football field. A team scores a touchdown when they reach the other team's end zone.

field goal: a kick between the upright posts that are at both ends of a football field. A field goal is worth three points.

goal line: a line that appears at both ends of a football field. To score a touchdown, a player must carry the ball across the goal line or pass the ball to a teammate in the end zone.

linebacker: a member of the defense who usually plays in the middle of the field

playoffs: a series of games held to determine a champion

quarterback: a player whose main job is to throw passes

rivals: teams that compete against one another for the same prize

rookies: first-year players

running back: a player whose main job is to run with the ball

rushing: running with the ball

scholarship: money awarded to students to help pay for college

scouts: football experts who watch players closely to judge their abilities

wide receiver: a player whose main job is to catch passes

Further Reading & Websites

Kennedy, Mike, and Mark Stewart. *Touchdown: The Power and Precision of Football's Perfect Play*. Minneapolis: Millbrook Press, 2010.

Buffalo Bills Website
http://www.buffalobills.com
The official website of the Bills includes team schedules, news, profiles of past and present players and coaches, and much more.

NFL Website
http://www.nfl.com
The NFL's official website provides fans with recent news stories, statistics, biographies of players and coaches, and information about games.

The Official Website of LeSean McCoy
http://www.leseanmccoy25.com
Visit this website to learn all about what's happening in the life of LeSean McCoy.

Sports Illustrated Kids
http://www.sikids.com
The *Sports Illustrated Kids* website covers all sports, including football.

LERNER

SOURCE

Expand learning beyond the printed book. Download free, complementary educational resources for this book from our website, www.lernerresource.com.

Index

Photo Acknowledgments

The images in this book are used with the permission of: AP Photo/Damian Strohmeyer, pp. 4, 6; © Ron Jenkins/Forth Worth Star-Telegram/TNS/Getty Images, p. 5; AP Photo/Tim Sharp, p. 7; AP Photo/John F. Rhodes, p. 8; AP Photo/Tim Sharp, p. 9; © Philip Scalia/Alamy, p. 10; © VanHart/Shutterstock.com, p. 11; © John Biever/Sports Illustrated/Getty Images, p. 14; © Dilip Vishwanat/Getty Images, p. 15; © Lee Martin/Alamy, p. 16; © George Gojkovich/Getty Images, p. 18; AP Photo/Jeff Gentner, p. 19; AP Photo/Don Wright, p. 20; AP Photo/Lynne Sladky, p. 22; AP Photo/Matt Slocum, pp. 23, 24; © Ronald Martinez/Getty Images, p. 25; AP Photo/Paul Spinelli, p. 26; AP Photo/Gary Wiepert, p. 27; AP Photo/Matt Rourke, p. 28; AP Photo/Brian Garfinkel, p. 29.

Front cover: AP Photo/Gary Wiepert.

Main body text set in Caecilia LT Std 55 Roman 16/28.
Typeface provided by Adobe Systems.